D1544817

DANGER LINES
IN THE
DEEPER LIFE

Danger Lines in the Deeper Life

A.B. SIMPSON

CHRISTIAN PUBLICATIONS
CAMP HILL, PENNSYLVANIA

Christian Publications
3825 Hartzdale Drive, Camp Hill, PA 17011

The mark of 🕇 *vibrant faith*

ISBN: 0-87509-440-6
LOC Catalog Card Number: 90-84957
© 1991 by Christian Publications
All rights reserved
Printed in the United States of America

91 92 93 94 95   5 4 3 2 1

Cover Photo: Michael Saunier

#24319876

CONTENTS

The Cause of Spiritual Failure

And they called that place Bokim. (Judges 2:5)

The book of Judges has an important place in the plan of divine revelation. It expresses a great truth and teaches a deep and solemn lesson: the danger of spiritual declension after great spiritual blessing.

The book of Numbers is a sad book, because it tells of the wanderings of Israel in the wilderness for 40 years after God brought the people out of Egypt. But Judges is a sadder and more solemn book—it tells of the failure of Israel after they had entered the Land of Promise, a failure that lasted not 40 years but 400. It represents the danger of backsliding after a person has received the Holy Spirit and known Jesus in His fullness— a danger most real and alarming. The author of Hebrews warns against the same thing: "We want each of you to show this same diligence to the very end, in order to make your hope sure" (6:11).

There is a place in the discipline of the Christian life and in the wise and faithful dealing of God with His people for both warning and promise, for both hope and fear. No one is so unsafe as he who recklessly dreams of safety without vigilance and obedience. God has planted beacons all along the way, not to discourage us with needless fear, but to save us with wholesome caution and vigilant obedience.

Judges stands in a larger sense for the declension of the Church of Christ after the apostolic age, and it represents the dark ages of Christian history. But in its personal application it may also represent the danger of retreating from the baptism of Pentecost and the deepest and highest experiences of the Holy Spirit.

The book begins with a record of victory.

> After the death of Joshua, the Israelites asked the Lord, "Who will be the first to go up and fight for us against the Canaanites?"
>
> The Lord answered, "Judah is to go up; I have given the land into their hands."
>
> Then the men of Judah said to the Simeonites their brothers, "Come up with us into the territory allotted to us, to fight against the Canaanites. We in turn will go with you into yours." So the Simeonites went with them.
>
> When Judah attacked, the Lord gave the Canaanites and Perizzites into their hands and they struck down ten thousand men at Bezek. (1:1–4)

This episode demonstrated Israel's faith, obedience and humble dependence upon God. Further on we read that they even took Jerusalem and that they captured Hebron and other strongholds. They continued on to the country of the Philistines, driving them from most of their strongholds. It seemed as if they still possessed the victorious faith of Joshua and had in their midst the same Almighty Presence.

Indications of a coming failure

But we soon see indications of the coming failure. First, the men of Judah began to pause in their career of triumph. We read in verse 19: "they were unable to drive the people from the plains, because they had iron chariots." Then we read of the partial failure of the tribe of Benjamin, "The Benjamites, however, failed to dislodge the Jebusites, who were living in Jerusalem; to this day the Jebusites live there with the Benjamites" (verse 21). It was not that they "could not" dislodge them; they "did not."

Next we find that Manasseh failed to drive out the inhabitants of Beth Shan and the neighboring towns: "for the Canaanites were determined to live in that land" (verse 27). Ephraim too fails to drive out the Canaanites living in Gezer. And so it is with other of the Israelite leaders. There was hardly a tribe that did not, in some degree, compromise with the enemy and give place to the people God had sent them to destroy.

If we look at the above passage closely, we can

see the several steps of their failure. First, the Israelites simply let the enemy remain. They no doubt thought the Canaanites would pose no further threat.

Second, we find the Israelites deliberately putting the Canaanites under their control for the purpose of making a profit from them. This is where the world gets into our Christian lives today. We compromise with evil, not only allowing it but using it for our own purposes. We think there is no harm in taking money from wicked men for religious objects. We are willing to be agreeable to the world so that we can influence it. But in the end we fall completely under its power.

Third, we find the Canaanites living alongside the Israelites (verse 27). Then, a little later, we find Israel living with the Canaanites (verse 33). Israel began by treating the Canaanites as guests or slaves, but ended by finding that they had become their masters and conquerors.

Fourth, we see the Canaanites driving the children of Dan into the mountains. They grew strong enough to dictate and demand, as evil always does after we have given it standing room for a little while.

Fifth, God's people intermarried with the enemy. They met in the social intimacies of life. They found the people of the world agreeable and profitable, and they consented to the forbidden fellowships and intermarriages of the godly and the ungodly, which in every age have preceded a time of corruption and great wickedness. No child of God has any right to intermarry with the ungodly, and a true parent dare not consent to such a union without involving the eternal well-being of the child. (It is never safe to disobey God, and I have no hesitation in saying that I would not perform such a marriage ceremony.)

The sixth step was partnership in idolatry and the forsaking of Jehovah's worship for the rites of heathenism. In chapter 3 we read:

> They took their daughters in marriage and gave their own daughters to their sons, and served their gods.
>
> The Israelites did evil in the eyes of the Lord; they forgot the Lord their God and served the Baals and the Asherahs. (verses 6–7)

The culmination of all this was the anger of Jehovah and His severe and righteous judgment upon His disobedient people:

> In his anger against Israel the Lord handed them over to raiders who plundered them. He sold them to their enemies all around, whom they were no longer able to resist. Whenever Israel went out to fight, the hand of the Lord was against them to defeat them, just as he had sworn to them. They were in great distress. (2:14–15)

God hates sin

What a dreadful thing it is to have God against us and to know that He who controls the breath of our lives and all the elements of destruction around us is compelled by His nature to deal contrary to us and to consume us—even as fire consumes every combustible thing it touches! God is compelled to be against sin, and while He pities the sinner, He hates the sin. While we are against God, His presence must be to us a consuming fire. We would fly from the awful blaze of His holy glance as from a lightning flash and long to hide ourselves in hell.

But there is something even sadder than this. We read that God gave them up to the power of their enemies and allowed the Canaanites to be the thorns and snares of judgment and temptation to them.

There is nothing more terrible in all the judgments pronounced against Israel than this: "Now therefore I tell you that I will not drive them out before you; they will be thorns in your sides and their gods will be a snare to you" (2:3).

And later we read:

> Therefore the Lord was very angry with Israel and said, "Because this nation has violated the covenant that I laid down for their forefathers and has not listened to me, I will no longer drive out before them any of the nations Joshua left when he died. I will use

them to test Israel and see whether they will keep the way of the Lord and walk in it as their forefathers did. (2:20–21)

God allowed them to be filled with their own devices and tempted and tried by the results of their own disobedience. He even sold them into the hands of their enemies and gave their foes a power to subdue and enslave them, which they could have never claimed without divine permission. From that time forward, the Canaanites, Philistines, Assyrians, Babylonians and Romans were but the executioners of divine judgment. They succeeded in their conquests by God's permission.

God's last and most terrible judgment

All of this represents an awful truth: God's last and most terrible judgment is to allow the devil to have power over the disobedient soul and to permit temptation to overcome, torment and punish him because of his disobedience and rejection of the grace that would have saved him. The saddest thing about the condition of the sinner is that while he thinks he is free and has the power to reform and do as he pleases, he is the helpless slave of Satan. He can never be free until he repents and renounces the dominion of God's great enemy and appeals to the blood of Jesus Christ and the power of the Holy Spirit to break the fetters of his captivity.

There may come a time in the life of a wicked

man when, through persistent rejection of light and right, he shall be given over, as we read in Romans, "to a depraved mind," and "to shameful lusts" (1:26, 28). He shall find within him a power compelling him to evil and possessing him with the devil just as one can be possessed and constrained by the Holy Spirit.

This explains the hardening of Pharaoh's heart. It is the last stage of impenitence and despair, and it never comes to any person until he has rejected and refused the mercy of God and has deliberately chosen evil instead of good, Satan instead of God.

> Since they hated knowledge
>   and did not choose to fear the Lord,
> since they would not accept my advice,
>   and spurned my rebuke,
> they will eat the fruit of their ways
>   and be filled with the fruit of their own
>   schemes.
>   (Proverbs 1:29–31)

It is possible even for the child of God to be delivered over to the power of temptation through a continuance in willful and persistent disobedience. The things that we choose become our punishment, and through our own deliberate disobedience, we find ourselves under temptation that we cannot resist. The reason is that we are in a place where God never wanted us to be. We have brought upon ourselves our own torment.

The grace of God is equal to all His will for us, and He knows how to deliver the godly out of temptation. But He has not promised His grace for self-imposed burdens, dangers or situations that are contrary to His divine purpose.

There is nothing sweeter in life than to be conscious of being so encased in the armor of the Holy Spirit that Satan cannot touch us. Every fiery shot glances off, and we walk through the hosts of hell as safe and unscathed as if we were treading the courts of heaven.

But there is also an experience where we are conscious that Satan has a power over our hearts; that the fiery darts do penetrate and stain the sensitive soul; that the evil instigation does become a part of our thoughts and feelings; and that we are not in perfect victory over the power of evil. This is the meaning of the Master's prayer: "Lead us not into temptation, / but deliver us from the evil one" (Matthew 6:13).

This is the meaning of hell, the beginning of torment, the retribution of sin. This is something even more bitter than the wrath of God. It is the culmination of the first step of unbelief, disobedience and spiritual declension. Let us guard against the first step, and let us ask Him to save us from the causes that led His people of old into these depths of wretchedness and sin.

Incomplete and unfinished work

The first cause was incomplete and unfinished work. The Israelites did not finish the task. They compromised with evil. Let us make sure that we give no place to the devil and that we allow the world and the flesh no standing ground. All Satan asks is toleration of a single root of bitterness, unbelief or self-indulgence. As surely as God is true, however, that single sin will destroy us in the end.

Second, the Israelites failed to recognize their temptations as God's tests. He allowed the things to come so that He could prove their obedience. Similarly, He lets temptations come to us, not so that they may overcome us, but so that they can establish us. If we would recognize them as God's tests and rise above them to meet His higher will, they would become occasions for grander victories and higher advances.

But the real secret of their failure was the lack of a true, personal and independent hold upon God as the Source of their strength. There is one passage in the opening verses of Judges that explains the situation: "The people served the Lord throughout the lifetime of Joshua and of the elders who outlived him and who had seen all the great things the Lord had done for Israel" (Judges 2:7).

The root of their problems

Here we see the cause of the whole trouble. The Israelites leaned upon Joshua and Joshua's immediate successors more than they leaned upon God. They got their ideas and inspiration from human leaders, but they did not stand personally rooted and grounded in God. When the shock of conflict came, they failed. Indeed, their own language on a previous occasion shows that they did not really understand their own helplessness and their utter need of Jehovah.

In the closing chapter of Joshua we read that when that great leader had gathered the people together at Shechem and given them his parting charges, they answered with unreserved assurance, " 'We too will serve the Lord, because he is our God.' Joshua said to the people, 'You are not able to serve the Lord' " (Joshua 24:18–19).

What Joshua meant was that they could not in their self-confident strength do anything but fail and sin. They had not learned the lesson, and confident in their self-sufficiency, they did fail and sink into the depth of sin and misery. The triumphs of Jericho, Bethoron, Hebron and Gibeon ended in the tears of Bokim and captivity by their foes.

Thank God there is another side to Bokim, the place of which the inspired prophet said, "No longer will they call you Deserted, / or name your land Desolate. / But you will be called Hephzibah, / and your land Beulah" (Isaiah 62:4). Bokim is the place of weeping; Beulah is the place of love and joy. Bokim means failure of our strength; Beulah means married to Him and kept by His power from stumbling and from failure.

Let us go to Bokim and learn our helplessness. And then let us go forth to Beulah and, leaning upon His love and strength, go forward, singing:

"But thanks be to God! He gives us the victory through our Lord Jesus Christ" (1 Corinthians 15:57). "I can do everything through him who gives me strength" (Philippians 4:13).

Sinning and Repenting

In his anger against Israel the Lord handed them over to raiders who plundered them. He sold them to their enemies all around, whom they were no longer able to resist. Whenever Israel went out to fight, the hand of the Lord was against them to defeat them, just as he had sworn to them. They were in great distress.

Then the Lord raised up judges, who saved them out of the hands of these raiders. Yet they would not listen to their judges but prostituted themselves to other gods and worshiped them. Unlike their fathers, they quickly turned from the way in which their fathers had walked, the way of obedience to the Lord's commands. Whenever the Lord raised up a judge for them, he was with the judge and saved them out of the hands of their enemies as long as the judge lived; for the Lord had compassion on them as they groaned under those who oppressed and afflicted them. But when the judge died, the people returned to ways even more corrupt than those of their fathers, following other gods and serving and worshiping them. They refused to give up their evil practices and stubborn ways. (Judges 2:14–19)

This is the story of the whole book of Judges—sinning and repenting. And it can be seen as a picture of the Church and the Christian when they fall into a state of rebellion.

What made Israel's rebellion worse, though, was that it followed a period of spiritual blessing. It came not as the wandering in the wilderness did, after their deliverance from Egypt. But it came after their victorious entrance into Canaan and their enjoyment of the life of victory and the fullness of God's blessing.

Its historical parallel is the story of the Dark Ages in the history of Christianity, when for centuries the Church sank into apostasy and worldliness, and for a thousand years the light of truth and holiness was almost wholly blotted out. It has its individual parallel in the experience of the child of God, when, after the baptism of the Holy Spirit, he or she falls back into spiritual declension and disobedience and returns to a life of sinning and repenting.

The progression of evil—and of grace

Let us look at how God dealt with this sinful people. First, we read the story of Othniel:

> The Israelites did evil in the eyes of the Lord; they forgot the Lord their God and served the Baals and the Asherahs. The anger of the Lord burned against Israel so that he sold them into the hands of Cushan-

Rishathaim king of Aram Naharaim, to whom the Israelites were subject for eight years. But when they cried out to the Lord, he raised up for them a deliverer, Othniel son of Kenaz, Caleb's younger brother, who saved them. The Spirit of the Lord came upon him, so that he became Israel's judge and went to war. The Lord gave Cushan-Rishathaim king of Aram into the hands of Othniel, who overpowered him. So the land had peace for forty years, until Othniel son of Kenaz died. (Judges 3:7–11)

Next, is the story of Ehud:

Once again the Israelites did evil in the eyes of the Lord, and because they did this evil the Lord gave Eglon king of Moab power over Israel. Getting the Ammonites and Amalekites to join him, Eglon came and attacked Israel, and they took possession of the City of Palms. The Israelites were subject to Eglon king of Moab for eighteen years.

Again the Israelites cried out to the Lord, and he gave them a deliverer—Ehud, a left-handed man, the son of Gera the Benjamite. The Israelites sent him with tribute to Eglon king of Moab. Now Ehud had made a double-edged sword about a foot and a half long, which he strapped to his right thigh under his clothing. He presented the tribute to Eglon king of Moab, who was a very fat man. After Ehud had presented the tribute, he sent on their way the men who had carried it. At the idols near Gilgal he himself turned back and said, "I have a secret message for you, O king."

The king said, "Quiet!" And all his attendants left him.

Ehud then approached him while he was sitting alone in the upper room of his summer palace and said, "I have a message from God for you." As the king rose from his seat, Ehud reached with his left hand, drew the sword from his right thigh and plunged it into the king's belly. Even the handle sank in after the blade, which came out his back. Ehud did not pull the sword out, and the fat closed in over it. Then Ehud went out to the porch; he shut the doors of the upper room behind him and locked them.

After he had gone, the servants came and found the doors of the upper room locked. They said, "He must be relieving himself in the inner room of the house." They waited to the point of embarrassment, but when he did not open the doors of the room, they took a key and unlocked them. There they saw their lord fallen to the floor, dead.

While they waited, Ehud got away. He passed by the idols and escaped to Seirah. When he arrived there, he blew a trumpet in the hill country of Ephraim, and the Israelites went down with him from the hills, with him leading them.

"Follow me," he ordered, "for the Lord has given Moab, your enemy, into your hands." So they followed him down and, taking possession of the fords of the Jordan that led to Moab, they allowed no one to cross over. At that time they struck down about ten thousand Moabites, all vigorous and strong; not a man escaped. That day Moab was made subject to Israel, and the land had peace for eighty years. (Judges 3:12–30)

These two incidents, following each other in direct succession, illustrate the progression of evil—and the progression of God's grace.

We cannot fail to notice here the aggravation of repeated sin. We read in verse 7 that "the Israelites did evil in the eyes of the Lord." And we read the same thing in verse 12: "the Israelites did evil in the eyes of the Lord." In the second passage, however, we see that the effects of their sin were much more serious the second time.

After their first disobedience we are told that God sold them into the hands of the enemy, and they served them eight years. Now, God not only gives them into the hands of the enemy, but He gives "Eglon king of Moab power over Israel." And this time they served the enemy 18 years!

Here we find God working on the side of Israel's enemies, giving them power to afflict His people. We see that the effect of continued sin is to prolong the period of our chastisement and fix the habit of evil until it becomes almost permanent. It is an awful truth that evil men and women grow worse and worse, and the power of sin to hurt them and to hold them increases with every repetition. It was not merely that God prolonged the Israelites captivity by His arbitrary will, but it seems as if they themselves had been so paralyzed by their sin and judgment, that they did not even think of turning to Him for help for 18 years.

A long-suffering God

We cannot doubt that God always listened to Israel when they cried to Him. But the saddest effect of their sin was that they forgot His former mercy and failed to lift up to Him their penitent cry. Over against their sin, though, is the mercy of a long-suffering God! The moment they turned to Him in prayer and penitence, He heard their cry and sent them help. How striking is the expression, "Again the Israelites cried out to the Lord, and he gave them a deliverer." His mercy was instant, and His deliverance was complete.

And the duration of the blessing was in proportion to the length of the judgment. When He saved them from the captivity of Cushan-Rishathaim, eight years long, He gave them rest for 40 years. When He saved them from the captivity of Eglon, 18 years long, He gave them rest for 80 years. It would seem as if His mercy was graduated in contrast to their sorrows and their sin. The days of blessing were more than four times as long as the days of punishment and pain.

Has God caused you to look back at some dark chapter of backsliding and spiritual loss? If so, take comfort from the story of Israel's sin. Turn to God in true-hearted repentence and obedience, and He "will repay you for the years the locusts have eaten— / the great locust and the young locust, / and the other locusts and the locust swarm— / my great army that I sent among you" (Joel 2:25).

How beautiful to observe in the story of Simon Peter that when the Lord restored him after his threefold sin, He gave him a threefold blessing and commission—as if He would put a mark of honor over against every scar that the disciple had brought upon himself. "Make us glad for as many days as you have afflicted us, / for as many years as we have seen trouble" (Psalm 90:15).

That is the mercy of God. But how much better and sweeter is the grace of God that is able "to keep [us] from falling and to present [us] before his glorious presence without fault and with great joy" (Jude 24).

A superficial experience

There are some further lessons in connection with these incidents that are worth examining. Notice how all through this period the people were dependent upon human leaders. They were faithful to God as long as Joshua lived, but they had no direct dependence on Joshua's God.

Theirs was a reflected goodness, derived from the circumstances and the people that surrounded them. They were true to God while their judge led them on to victory and ruled over them afterward. But when he died, their hearts, like the sapling that has only been bent, sprang back again to their natural willfulness: "the people returned to ways even more corrupt . . . following other gods and serving and worshiping them. They refused to give up their evil practices and stubborn ways" (Judges 2:19).

This is the whole root of bitterness—a superficial experience influenced by persons and circumstances, while the natural heart still remains and is not personally united to the Lord Jesus Christ and filled with His Spirit. The promise of this dispensation, thank God, is not that we shall have Othniels and Ehuds, Joshuas and Calebs to lead us, but that the Holy Spirit shall be poured out "on all people" (Acts 2:17), and "no longer will a man teach his neighbor / or a man his brother, saying, 'Know the Lord,' / because they will all know me, / from the least of them to the greatest" (Jeremiah 31:34).

Patterns to follow

We are not, therefore, to look for our spiritual examples in the condition of the people of Israel. We should look for them in their leaders. These men were patterns of what each of us may be today in the power of the Holy Spirit.

In Othniel we see, according to the literal meaning of his name, the lion-hearted man, the man of faith and holy courage. We have heard of him before. It was he who, at Caleb's challenge, had dared to assault the stronghold of Kiriath Sepher (Judges 1:12). As a reward for his victory, Othniel won the hand of Achsah, the daughter of Caleb, whose name means "grace." And with her he received a dowry of special grace and blessing.

Othniel stands for the faith that in the first lessons of our Christian life dares to take the victory and receives the fullness of grace. And then, later, when others need our help, we are prepared to lead them into the same victory that we have won.

There is a story behind every story. There is a life behind every public record of triumph and distinction. The Othniel who led Israel to victory against the mighty emperor of the East was not the creation of a moment or the accident of a great occasion. He was the outgrowth and development of a long-past history, when as a young man he met the crisis hour of his own life and dared to believe God and overcome his enemies in the strength of the Lord. He won the blessing that enabled him to meet the greater occasion and to stand as the first of Israel's judges and conquerors.

His story is an example of what we will encounter. There will come a moment when we meet life's issues all alone, and as we stand true and triumph over self and sin, God's mark is placed upon us. He puts us aside for the day when He will need a brave leader and a chosen instrument for some of the great occasions of the world's history. And it will be found true again, as it ever has been true, that "the Lord has set apart the godly for himself" (Psalm 4:3).

A divinely appointed judge

The implication for us from the second account is not quite so clear as the first. Ehud is sent to assassinate the king of Moab. After bringing a tribute to the king, he gains his favor. He then tells the king he has a secret message for him. The king grants him a private audience, and Ehud tells him it is a message from God. Then he stabs the king with a sword he had hidden, killing his country's oppressor.

Many commentators have tried to excuse Ehud's act, or at least to exonerate God from all responsibility for it, by calling attention to the fact that it is not said, as in the case of Othniel, that the Spirit of God came upon Ehud. They seem disposed to apologize for him or to make him responsible for his own act, leaving it as a doubtful thing. But a candid reader cannot fail to notice that the inspired writer made no such attempt to evade responsibility. He frankly speaks of Ehud as the deliverer whom God raised up to save His people. He further recognized his whole career as that of a divine leader and judge.

How then shall we justify his act of apparent

murder? Surely, the answer is plain. It was not Ehud's act; it was not an act of private vengeance or even patriotic fervor. The answer is found in Ehud's message to Eglon: "I have a message from God to you" (verse 20). He was acting as a divinely appointed judge and executioner of God's sentence against a wicked and condemned man. Ehud acted by divine command and in the divine name. His victim stands before us as the type of our spiritual oppressor. And Ehud stands as the example of the faith that meets the enemy, not in its own name or strength, but in the name and strength of Jehovah, triumphing even as He did.

An inspiring lesson

There is an inspiring lesson in this attitude. Is it not our privilege to identify ourselves with God in all we say and do, to go forth in victory in His name? Is not this the meaning of that strong expression, "whatever you do, whether in word or deed, do it all in the name of the Lord Jesus" (Colossians 3:17)?

As we pray, for example, let us identify ourselves with Him until it shall not be our prayer, but God's prayer in us, and we shall know that the answer must be given. As we are tempted let us meet the devil as a conquered foe, and standing in the Person of our victorious Lord, let us say to him, "I have a message from God for you. He bids you flee. Get behind me, Satan, in the name of Jesus."

As we are called to speak let it be not our message, but His; not our ideas and opinions and pleadings, but the word from the throne, delivered to men with the authority of God. Let us look into their conscience and say in the name of our Master, "I have a message from God for you." Our words will be clothed with power, and the Holy Spirit will convict men of sin and righteousness and judgment and seal our message with precious souls and lasting fruits.

This is the true spirit of ministry: "If anyone speaks, he should do it as one speaking the very words of God. If anyone serves, he should do it with the strength God provides, so that in all things God may be praised through Jesus Christ" (1 Peter 4:11).

Conquer through Faith

And what more shall I say? I do not have time to tell about Gideon, Barak, Samson, Jephthah, David, Samuel and the prophets, who through faith conquered kingdoms, administered justice, and gained what was promised; who shut the mouths of lions, quenched the fury of the flames, and escaped the edge of the sword; whose weakness was turned to strength; and who became powerful in battle and routed foreign armies. (Hebrews 11:32–34; compare with Judges 3:31 and 4:14–15)

The darkness of night allows us to see the stars. Similarly, it seems that the darkest times of national and church history are always occasions for the best types of genius and character to shine. The long, sad story of the judges revealed a Deborah and a Barak, a Gideon and a Samson, an Othniel and a Jephthah. The times of Ahab and Jezebel were made illustrious by the ministry of Elijah and Elisha. The dark night of the Middle Ages was made luminous by the testimony of a Wycliffe, a Luther and a Knox.

Shamgar and an oxgoad

Shamgar's story is short. He is mentioned in only two verses: Judges 3:31 and 5:6. But we can learn much from his shining example.

"After Ehud came Shamgar son of Anath, who struck down six hundred Philistines with an oxgoad. He too saved Israel" (3:31). An oxgoad was a long, wooden rod that was often tipped with a piece of metal. It was used for driving draft animals. We are not sure of Shamgar's occupation, but we could assume that because he was carrying an oxgoad that he was a farmer.

Suddenly, he finds himself confronted by a large group of Philistines—possibly the precursors of another invasion of Israel. Seizing his oxgoad he strikes down 600 of the enemy. There can be no doubt but what his victory came with God's help. God took control of His chosen instrument and enabled him to defeat the Philistines—and save his country.

From this last phrase we can assume that Shamgar's encounter had a major impact on his country's history. No doubt the surviving Philistines went back to tell the tale of their strange disaster. No one would have dared to attack Israel after hearing how only one man routed an army.

Shamgar represents the spirit of Christian faith and victory. Here we see an ordinary man who met an emergency as it came to him without stepping aside from the path of ordinary duty. He did not need to mount a pedestal or be placed in some illustrious position to be a hero. He simply stood in the place where God put him and there became acclaimed through the force of his own personal character and conduct. He did not go out of his way to find a mission, but he met the events that came to him in the course of life, turning them into occasions for faith and victory.

He represents the men and women who stand in secular callings, and who find a pulpit and a ministry just where God has placed them, amid the tasks of daily life. He stands for the businessman at his office, who finds a thousand opportunities for fighting the battle of the Lord and doing good to his fellow men in the course of his routine.

I know a person who repairs shoes. Every day he finds in his shop a dozen opportunities for telling others about Jesus Christ. God has used him to lead many of his customers to the Person who transformed his own heart and life. I know too, a captain on a passenger ship who preaches the gospel in his plain and modest way to thousands of passengers every year. His cabin has been the birthplace of hundreds of Christians.

Our present resources

Shamgar did not have to wait until he had a sword or a spear or a battle-bow to fight. He took as a weapon the thing that was in his hand and turned it against the enemy. Similarly, God wants whatever resources that are at your disposal. He asks, "What is that in your hand?" (Exodus 4:2) and Moses' rod, Dorcas's needle, Shamgar's ox-goad, David's sling and stone, Joshua's ram's horn, the lad's five loaves and two fishes and the widow's little can of oil are all that He requires for His mightiest victories and His grandest ministries. Give Him what you have, be faithful where you are, do what you can and He will do the rest.

Shamgar's victory may seem small compared with Gideon's. If we just look at numbers, we could say that was true. But we have to see the larger picture. God used it to prevent a major invasion and to render needless some more costly victory afterward. Likewise, the little things we do, the faithfulness with which we meet some trifling opportunity, may prevent some greater disaster or be the occasion of some mightier blessing than we can see at the time.

It may seem a small thing for a woman on a dark and stormy night to dash along the railroad track and signal the rushing train to stop before it reaches the broken bridge, but that single act of heroism saved a hundred lives. It may seem a little thing for a small group of heroes to hold a pass against an army, but that was the key to the whole battle.

It may be a trifling thing for a quiet English girl to find a ragged street urchin and induce him to go to Sunday school by giving him a suit of clothes. Then, when he did not show up, she hunted him up weeks afterward and gave him another suit of clothes, only to find that he did not come to church. Refusing to be discouraged by the boy's deception, she found him a third time. Her patience triumphed and that boy was won for Christ.

To most it was a small thing; they surely felt the boy was not worth pursuing. But the day came when that act of tireless love was God's first step in the evangelization of China. That boy was Robert Morrison, the pioneer of modern missions in the Far East.

These are the little things that God loves to glorify! I pray that He will help us watch for those wayside opportunities and win those battles of faith and fortitude.

The ministry of a woman

Our next illustration is the story of Deborah and Barak. Here we are introduced to a new work of God—the ministry of a woman.

Deborah stands before us in strong contrast to the customs and prejudices of her time. She is called to lead in a national crisis, to stand in the front of both statesmanship and war as the head of the nation. This is an unqualified recognition of the part women play in ministry, and no man should deny the place of women in the history of nations and the ministries of Christianity.

At the same time, the story of Deborah gives no encouragement to the "new woman" in her absurd attempt to usurp the place of men. Christ has established the natural and spiritual law that the head of every woman is the man, and the head

of the man is Christ. This is the type of woman-
hood that Deborah represented.

Though she knew that she was called by her
spiritual qualifications to lead her people to
deliverance from the enemy, Deborah took particular pains to find a man to be the executive of-
ficer of her plans and the leader of God's hosts in
the divine campaign. Her chief business was to
put Barak in the front, and then stand by him
with her counsel, prayers, faith and wholesome
reproof.

Deborah was a practical and sensible woman.
Her name signifies "the bee," and she possessed
the sting as well as the honey. She knew how to
stir up Barak by wholesome severity as well as encourage him by holy inspiration. Her conclusions,
though not reasoned out so elaborately as a
man's, generally reached the right end by intui-
tions that were seldom wrong. She exhibited yiel-
dedness and love rather than dogmatism and
defiance.

But Barak was a foolish man who refused to be
helped by the shrewd, intuitive wisdom of a true
woman. We see in him a man of weak and timid
faith, losing much by his diffidence, and yet used
of God and lifted up by the inspiration of
Deborah.

Barak shrank at first from the unexpected call to
lead an army of 10,000 men against the large
army of Sisera. He finally consented when
Deborah agreed to go with him, but his timidity
cost him the honor he would have won: "But be-

cause of the way you are going about this, the honor will not be yours, for the Lord will hand Sisera over to a woman" (Judges 4:9).

Despite his hesitancy, God used Barak, and he became one of the shining stars of Jewish history mentioned in Hebrews. God can use the weakest instruments, and He generally does choose the poor in spirit and temperament to clothe in His supernal might.

> God chose the foolish things of the world to shame the wise; God chose the weak things of the world to shame the strong. He chose the lowly things of this world and the despised things—and the things that are not—to nullify the things that are, so that no one may boast before him. (1 Corinthians 1:27–29)

Look at Isaiah when God called him to his splendid ministry. How little he thought of himself. "Woe is me! . . . I am ruined! For I am a man of unclean lips," (Isaiah 6:5). Yet God used him to unfold the majestic visions of messianic prophecy.

Look at Jeremiah as he shrank back into his conscious nothingness, and cried, "Lord, I am a child," (Jeremiah 1:6). But God took that trembling reed and made him a pillar of strength and a fenced brazen wall of resistance against the kings, the prophets and the priests of Israel. He was the grandest figure of the last days of Jerusalem.

Yes, God can take us in our weakness and nothingness and make us strong in His might to the pulling down of strongholds.

So God took Barak in his weakness. He responded to the inspiring call of faith that counts the things that are not as though they were. "Go!" Deborah told him. "This is the day the Lord has given Sisera into your hands." She went on to say, as she counted the victory as already won, "Has not the Lord gone ahead of you?" (Judges 4:14). She committed the whole matter into Jehovah's hands and told Barak to simply follow on and take the victory that was already given.

Is it possible for faith to speak in plainer terms, or language to express with stronger emphasis the imperative mood and the present tense of that victorious faith to which nothing is impossible?

Cooperating instruments

Another lesson we see here is that of mutual service. This victory was not won by any a single individual, but God linked together, as He loves to do, many cooperating instruments in the accomplishment of His will. Deborah represents the spirit of faith and prophecy. Barak exemplifies obedience and executive energy. There were the noble men of Zebulun and Naphtali who jeopardized their lives, the martyrs of sacrifice who are the crowning glory of every great enterprise. And there was Jael, a poor woman out on the frontiers of Israel, who gave the finishing touch to the victory.

But we also see in this account the curse of neutrality. In the Song of Deborah we see the unfaithful, ignoble and indifferent ones who quietly looked on while the battle raged—not only missing their reward, but justly receiving the curse of God's displeasure and judgment.

The tribes of Reuben and Gad, from the east of the Jordan, and those of Dan and Asher, from along the coast, are rebuked for not responding to the battle call. They may have had good intentions, but they did nothing, and Deborah unleashes her fiery scorn at them, saying

> Why did you stay among the campfires
> to hear the whistling for the flocks?
> Gilead stayed beyond the Jordan.
> And Dan, why did he linger by the ships?
> Asher remained on the coast
> and stayed in his coves.
> (Judges 5:16–17)

God's mighty warfare is raging still. Let us beware lest we, too, hide in vain behind our littleness and meet at last the same curse the city of Meroz received because they refused to help fight:

> "Curse Meroz," said the angel of the Lord.
> "Curse its people bitterly,
> because they did not come to help the Lord,
> to help the Lord against the mighty."
> (Judges 5:23)

In these last days, when millions are dying without the gospel and the coming of our Master waits but a few short years, perhaps we shall hear Him say, "Curse the servant who refused to use his single talent and his single pound—because it was so small—to the help the Lord against the mighty."

The final thing we see in this scene is a pattern page from God's book of remembrance. Some day we shall read the other pages and find our names recorded either with the inhabitants of Meroz and Reuben or with the victors of faith who stood with Deborah and Barak in the battles of the Lord. Will we shine like stars in the night now and then like the sun in the kingdom of our Father?

The Strength of Weakness

God chose the foolish things of the world to shame the wise; God chose the weak things of the world to shame the strong. He chose the lowly things of this world and the despised things—and the things that are not—to nullify the things that are, so that no one may boast before him. (1 Corinthians 1:27–29)

When the angel of the Lord appeared to Gideon, he said, "The Lord is with you, mighty warrior."

The Lord turned to him and said, "Go in the strength you have and save Israel out of Midian's hand. Am I not sending you?"

The Lord said to Gideon, "You have too many men for me to deliver Midian into their hands." (Judges 6:12, 14; 7:2)

The strength of weakness leaning upon God, and the weakness of human strength—this is the paradox; this is the spiritual truth that Gideon's life illustrates.

We see this principle in Gideon's call. The angel of the Lord suddenly appeared before him with the startling greeting, "The Lord is with you, mighty warrior." Gideon no doubt felt as if he was anything but a mighty warrior, and we can imagine that his expression must have evidenced this. Immediately, he began to apologize and explain to the angel the helplessness and distress of his people.

But instead of the angel answering him, Gideon next heard the Lord speak: "Go in the strength you have and save Israel out of Midian's hand. Am I not sending you?" Gideon questioned God, saying his clan was the weakest in Israel and that he was the least in his family. Again the Lord told Gideon that He would be with him. And Gideon finally understood that it was not his strength that would save his country but God's. It was the strength of faith that is always the strength of weakness, because it is the strength of God.

A paradox to the natural mind

This is the story of grace and the secret of supernatural power. It is a paradox to the natural mind. "When I am weak, then am I strong," is the theme of every victorious saint.

God comes to the sinner and by a word of sovereign grace pronounces him forgiven, and that word makes him what it declares. He comes to the sinful person and says, "Now you are clean through the word that I have spoken to you," and that word creates the fact of his sanctification. He comes to the struggling Jacob and by a word transforms him into conquering Israel. He comes to the stormy Boanerges, and he is henceforth the gentle John. Grace speaks and it is done, and faith counts the things that are not as though they were.

We see this principle in the test of Gideon's faith as he is transformed from the natural man to the man of faith. But how weak his faith is, and how slowly it develops into maturity and confidence.

Doubting the authenticity of his supernatural visitor, Gideon asks for a sign. The angel agrees, and Gideon hurries off to prepare an offering. At the angel's request he places it on a rock. The angel reaches over and touches the offering with the tip of his staff, and immediately fire flares from the rock and consumes the meat and bread.

No sooner had Gideon's test been granted than he broke down with a cry of fear: "Ah, Sovereign Lord! I have seen the angel of the Lord face to face!" Once again, the Lord reassures Gideon, "Peace! Do not be afraid. You are not going to die" (Judges 6:22). So he built an altar to God and went forth to take his first step of faith and obedience.

This began at his own home, his father's house. His father had built an altar to Baal and an Asherah pole (a symbol of the goddess). God commanded Gideon to tear down the altar and cut down the pole and use the wood to build a proper altar to Him, offering up his father's second bullock.

Still we see the timid man and the trembling faith even in his obedience. He took 10 of his servants and, waiting until night, did as God told him. In the morning his neighbors looked with astonishment and anger upon the wreck of their shrine and the evidences of Gideon's bold rebellion. They soon found out who had committed this act, and their cries were loud and unanimous that he should die.

But Joash, Gideon's shrewd father, tactfully turned aside the anger of the people by suggesting that if Baal was a true God he would deal with Gideon himself. "If Baal really is a god, he can defend himself when someone breaks down his altar" (verse 31). The father's brave attitude turned the tide, and God sustained His obedient child, as He always will for those who trust in Him.

No sooner had Gideon begun his task than the devil began to stir up his forces. The Amalekites and Midianites assembled a mighty army and pitched their camp in the valley of Jezreel. Then the Spirit of God came upon Gideon, and he blew a mighty trumpet call to summon the people of his city, and his clan gathered around his standard. From Manasseh, Asher, Zebulun and Naphtali volunteers poured in, until Gideon stood at the head of an army of 32,000 men.

A reassuring sign

Again we see that Gideon's faith began to falter, and once more he came to Jehovah for a reassuring sign. God was gentle with his trembling servant; He saw the true purpose of obedience, and He gave him time to be sure. He always does.

When God commands us to take any important step, He always will grant us all the certainty and all the strength we need.

Gideon suggested that he would place a wool fleece on the threshing floor. If the next morning the fleece was wet with dew and the floor around it was dry, then he would know that God was going to save Israel by his hand.

The next morning Gideon went to the barn. He picked up the fleece and wrung a bowlful of water out of it. The ground all around was completely dry.

Still Gideon shrank from going forward. Once more he asked God to give him a sign—that the token of the previous night be reversed. The fleece should be dry and the ground wet with dew. Again God delivered the asked-for sign.

There was one good thing about Gideon's second request. He was willing to have his sign turned upside down. Sometimes when we are asking for guidance, we want it all one way, and this is usually the reason why we are so often misguided. We are biased in our preference. We want the dew always in our fleece, and we are not willing for it to be dry. But Gideon's will was so fully surrendered to God that he was ready to take His answer either way. As a result, God could teach him.

We have the Bible and the Holy Spirit

It is different for us today. God does not direct His children by this type of sign. He has given us

His Holy Word and His Holy Spirit to show us the way we ought to go.

We should be careful in resorting to deciding things by chance, or by opening our Bibles at random. We should shy away from a presumptuous and superstitious dependence upon omens and portents that have lead so many astray.

In the Bible we have a standard of right and wrong upon which we can always depend for general principles to direct our actions. In the voice of the Holy Spirit, we have the special guidance that we need in particular circumstances. But there are certain conditions that we must always observe: "He guides the humble in what is right / and teaches them his way" (Psalm 25:9). The yielded and willing person who chooses his or her own way and then comes to God to have Him endorse it, will be likely to go astray.

We know from reading the New Testament that the apostles, when there was an important decision to be made, gathered and prayed and waited for the Lord's direction. So the wise man today will always bring to every question not only the general principles of the Holy Scriptures and the special whisperings of the Holy Spirit, but also a sanctified judgment and a calm, deliberate consideration of all the circumstances and providences concerned. He will then hold these humbly before the Lord in prayer, suspending all action until impressions become absolute convictions. At that time, he can go forth with certainty and rest to follow the path that has been indicated and leave the results with God.

Listen and obey along the way

Next, we see the principle of our text illustrated in the selection of Gideon's men. It was a good thing for Gideon that he was weak and timid enough to wait at every point for God's next word. It is quite possible for us to receive a command from the Lord and then to go forward blindly to obey it and really find ourselves at last out of step with God's order. Even though we were seeking to obey Him, we were failing because we did not stop and listen along the way for His further orders.

God guides us step by step and day by day. And it is necessary for us at every moment to listen and obey. Had Gideon gone out with his 32,000 men and all the trappings of a large army—floating banners, blaring trumpets and patriotic enthusiasm—he would surely have been defeated, and all God's promises would have failed. But he wisely waited for his Leader to point every step of the way.

We do have a manual of instructions in the Bible, but we also have a living Lord, a Leader to help us carry out our instructions. Let us walk closely with Him. For while with one breath He says, "Obey everything I have commanded you," in the other He says, "And surely I am with you always, to the very end of the age" (Matthew 28:20).

This is the mistake the Church has often made: it has taken a set of doctrines and rules and bound them up in a volume of instructions, principles, rules, creeds, confessions and doctrinal principles, and then gone forth to carry them out itself. We have no hesitation in saying that even the Bible without the Holy Spirit is not sufficient for the true Christian.

Sifting out

As Gideon waited on God, another message came: "You have too many men for me to deliver Midian into their hands" (Judges 7:2). So God began to sift them, and as Gideon watched, his splendid army melted away until two out of three had gone back at the bidding of their fears.

Similarly, God tests us and lets us retire from the tasks for which He knows we are inadequate. God lets us abandon them because He sees that we are afraid and would fail. But had we dared more, we might have had more.

But even the 10,000 men that were left were still too many for Gideon to accomplish his task. So there was a second test, and God thinned the group even further. How solemn it is to know that in every step we take, we are weighing our own lives, writing our own record and fixing our own place of service and reward!

Gideon brought his men to a brook and simply watched while they drank. Most of them, intent only upon drinking, knelt down and drank as a dog would, lapping the water with their tongues.

They never gave a second's thought that the enemy might be waiting to attack them. These men would not do for God's work, so He put them aside.

But there were a few, 300, who drank in a different fashion. With eyes alert, they brought handfuls of water up to their mouths. They satisfied their thirst, but they also remained alert against a surprise attack. These were God's men, and Gideon set them aside while the others went home with the timid ones.

How solemn, how true this is for you and for me! God is always bringing us to the valley of decision, to the test place of life. He gives us some blessing, some water from the fountain of love and prosperity, and He watches to see how we will drink. Often, we become so absorbed in the blessing that we forget everything else. By doing that, we show where our hearts really are, and God cannot trust us in His enterprises.

Perhaps He gives you money, and immediately you become absorbed in business or pleasure. Then when He calls with a sudden emergency, you are not ready. Perhaps He gives you a friend, and that friend becomes more to you than Christ or the call to duty. Perhaps it is some special service that is the test. He lets you disciple a new Christian or gives you a special position, but you become so absorbed in the task that you cannot hear His voice or watch His hand or be adjustable to His will. As a result of your failure, He has to set you aside, not from heaven, perhaps, but from

His highest will. He says, "Go home, drink all you want to. Sleep on now, and take your rest, the opportunity is passed."

Weighed in the balance

Oh, how the days are telling! Oh, how God is testing! Oh, how unconsciously to ourselves, each of us is being weighed in the balance! God help us to be watchful, to walk circumspectly, not as fools, but as wise men, redeeming the time, because the days are evil.

God does not give us notice of these tests before they come. This is an examination where the questions are not submitted to the candidates beforehand. We understand it all afterward, and how we wish that we had watched. The testing is not only for rewards of glory, but it is for the sake of higher service here. "If a man cleanses himself from the latter [from ignoble purposes], he will be made holy, useful to the Master and prepared to do any good work" (2 Timothy 2:21).

I heard a phrase that well illustrates Gideon's story. It was the expression, "out and out." God wants us to be "out and out." Gideon's men were "out and out." First, they were picked out from the 32,000. Then they were picked out from the 10,000.

So today God is picking out a people from even His professed followers. And from these, yes, even from the consecrated ones, He is picking those who have not only received the Holy Spirit, but have followed Him through all the tests and all the deaths, all the way, so that He can say of them, as we read of the followers of the Lamb in the day of His appearing, "and with him will be his called, chosen and faithful followers" (Revelation 17:14).

The Weapons of Our Warfare

The weapons we fight with are not the weapons of the world. On the contrary, they have divine power to demolish strongholds. (2 Corinthians 10:4)

The three companies blew the trumpets and smashed the jars. Grasping the torches in their left hands and holding in their right hands the trumpets they were to blow, they shouted, "A sword for the Lord and for Gideon!" While each man held his position around the camp, all the Midianites ran, crying out as they fled. (Judges 7:20–21)

This is the crowning illustration of the lesson of Gideon's life, the strength of weakness. In the weapons of Gideon's warfare as well as in Gideon and his followers, we see how God can use the weak things of this world to confound the strong. We see how He uses the things that are not to bring to nothing the things that are (1 Corinthians 1:27–28).

Before the assault we again see the timidity of Gideon. And God sees it too. He tells Gideon,

> Get up, go down against the camp, because I am going to give it into your hands. If you are afraid to attack, go down to the camp with your servant Purah and listen to what they are saying. Afterward you will be encouraged to attack the camp.
> (Judges 7:9–11).

We see that God encouraged the trembling faith of His child by giving him another sign. Stealthily, Gideon and his servant crept down to the edge of the Midianite camp, arriving just in time to hear one of the soldiers telling his friend about a dream he had. "A round loaf of barley came tumbling into the Midianite camp," the man said. "It struck the tent with such force that the tent overturned and collapsed" (verse 13).

The man's friend immediately interpreted the dream. "This can be nothing other than the sword of Gideon son of Joash, the Israelite. God has given the Midianites and the whole camp into his hands" (verse 14). That was enough to satisfy Gideon that God was already working. The enemies' fears were prophetic of their fate.

Likewise, God is working for those who trust Him. He can fight our battles for us in the hearts of our enemies and strike fear in them before the conflict begins. Let us have the faith to recognize our unseen Ally and the forces and resources that are waiting at His command to assist those who trust and obey Him.

The person you want to see accept Jesus as his

Savior is no doubt being prepared, through a series of divine providences, to listen to your words. When Elisha stood at Dothan surrounded by Syrian armies, it seemed to his frightened servant that all was lost. But there were armies in the sky and on the mountain tops ready to fight the battle for him.

In Gideon's case we see faith that reckons on the unseen and steps out into the darkness alone with God to find that He is just as able to turn the Midianites against each other as to strike them down by His sword. Indeed, He was already beginning to melt their hearts like wax and prepare them by their dreams for the panic and disaster that was to follow.

It mattered not that Gideon had only 300 men and that the enemy had 135,000. It did not matter that their weapons were lamps, pitchers and trumpets, for they did not need to strike a blow in this great battle. Jehovah was going to turn the Midianites against the Amalekites, while Gideon's army stood waving the torch and blowing the trumpet of victory, shouting, "For the Lord and for Gideon!" (verse 18). These simple and apparently foolish weapons are fitting for our warfare, too.

The pitcher

The pitcher was a clay vessel. It did not need to be strong or beautiful. If it had been made of iron or of brass, it would have been useless. Its fragility was its best attribute, because it was of no use until it was broken. How well it represents our bodies, vessels of clay as it were, through which God is pleased to work and about which He says, "Offer yourselves to God, . . . and offer the parts of your body to him as instruments of righteousness" (Romans 6:13). These members of our body are represented here as weapons. Our hands, feet, lips, eyes, ears and physical senses are all weapons to be used against evil and for the Lord.

Gideon's vessels had to be empty. Similarly, God requires our bodies and spirits to be given to Him exclusively and to be emptied of all our selfish desires, ready at any moment for His use and service. Then, when they are filled with His indwelling life and broken like Gideon's pitchers so that the light may shine through, God will use them in their weakness for the revelation of His glory and the accomplishment of His plans.

We need not be troubled about the breaking of the pitchers. God will do that or, at least, will allow it to be done. The circumstances and trials that come to us will furnish the occasion for the victory of His grace. I have seen a child of God standing unmoved amid intense provocation. The natural impulse would have been to speak out and take action. But instead there was a gentle silence and a sweet smile.

And what was the result? A strong man was broken by that victory of love and led to seek the grace that enabled that Christian to triumph over unkindness.

God lets these things come into our lives so

that we may reveal the light of His grace and the Spirit of Him whose agony in Gethsamane and shame upon the cross were but the background on which the glory of His grace shone out with a luster transcending even the transfiguration light.

The lamps

Gideon's lamps represented not only the light of truth and the source of all light, the Holy Spirit, but they also stood for the light of the indwelling Christ. The lamps were inside the pitchers, and Christ must be in us if we would shine. I have heard that travelers in the Arctic can take a piece of ice and shape it so that the sun's rays can be concentrated to start a fire. Unfortunately, the same is not true for human hearts. We must be on fire for God before we can set others on fire.

> Thou must thyself be true,
>   If thou the truth would'st teach.
> Thy heart must overflow, if thou
>   Another heart would'st reach.

"You are the light of the world," Jesus tells us (Matthew 5:14). It is not what we say, but what we are and what Christ is within us that constitutes the strength of our testimony and the power of our life. It is the life of Christ within us shining out that most honors God and most effectively works for His kingdom and glory.

The trumpets

The trumpet represents the gospel message. The trumpet of the Old Testament was not used as a musical instrument. It had no fine inflections of tone or sweet cadences of elocution. No, its sound was loud, and when people heard it, they knew that something was about to happen.

The word from which "preaching" comes is based on this figure: the trumpet of the herald. When Christ sent out His disciples to preach, He did not say, "Go, and give eloquent orations and artistic speeches." No, He said, "Go, and proclaim as a herald the glad tidings of salvation."

Likewise, our message should be as clear and as urgent as the herald's trumpet. And it should be so simple that no one can misunderstand it. This was what John the Baptist said he was, "A voice."

This is the chief business of missionaries. Let us not be misled by our own reasonings. Let us not be led into believing that we are sent overseas simply to gather about us bands of little children and to train them in the truths of Christianity, thus gradually preparing a Christian community, giving up as hopeless those who are more mature in years and more steeped in sin. God sends us to all men to flash before them the light of the living Christ and proclaim in their ears the message of God, believing that He who spoke to Midian's myriads in their dreams and filled their hearts with fear, can still speak to the hearts of men and arouse them to repentance and obedience by the power of the Holy Spirit.

Let this be the aim of our work and the claim of our faith, and we shall still find that the weapons of our warfare are as mighty as Gideon's. We need not be "ashamed of the gospel, because it is the power of God for the salvation of everyone who believes: first for the Jew, then for the Gentile" (Romans 1:16).

The battle cry

The battle cry of Gideon's band is full of instructive meaning. "For the Lord and for Gideon!"—what a startling battle cry! These were pointed and forceful words. How they must have rung out at that midnight hour! And what shrieks and groans of the terrified and wounded men answered them!

These were fitting watchwords, linking together divine operation and human cooperation. God comes first, for the battle is the Lord's. It is He who strikes down the enemy. It is He who uses and prepares the instrument. It is He who turns foes upon each other and fills their hearts with fear, deciding the battle before it even begins. It is He who is still present in all His unchanged omnipotence, who looks for opportunities to show Himself upright on behalf of those whose hearts are perfect toward Him.

It is He who sanctifies us, who is our Healer and Deliverer in temporal distress. It is He who, as the God of providence, still works in the events and circumstances of life in answer to His people's prayers. It is He who sits upon the throne—an everpresent God, making all things work together for good to them who love Him (Romans 8:28). It is He who by the Holy Spirit convicts the world of sin, of righteousness and of judgment (John 16:8).

He can break the hardest heart. He can change the most stubborn will. He can break down the iron walls of Hindu caste and bring tribes and nations to seek and acknowledge Him. He changed the persecuting Saul into a humble apostle of Jesus Christ. He can prompt the hearts of men to lay their treasures at His feet for the needed resources for the work of the gospel and the evangelization of the world.

He does not need our religious tricks or our shameful compromises with the world in order to gain the favor of the rich and win the popularity of the crowd. Christianity is supernatural power, and the same God who led Israel with pillar of cloud and fire, who spoke at Pentecost through the tongues of flame, who opened Peter's prison door, is waiting to work the greater wonders of His grace for us. Oh, for the sword of God! Oh, for the faith to claim it! Oh, for the proof of the promise, "Commit your way to the Lord; / trust in him and he will do this" (Psalm 37:5)!

There is Gideon's sword, too. There is a place for man's obedience as well as for man's faith. So Gideon must be true, and his 300 men must be adjusted and ready. They must follow him just as closely as he followed Jehovah. His command was urgent, "Watch me, . . . Follow my lead" (Judges 7:17). There must be perfect unity and precision of action.

There is not much for us to do, but what He does ask us to do, we should do and do it exactly as He says. And then, when the victory is won, there is still something to do. The foe must be followed up and pursued; the battle must be completed; the enemy must be cut off in its retreat.

God, teach us to trust as if all depended upon You, and to obey as if all depended upon us.

Self-renunciation
and
Self-aggrandizement

I have been crucified with Christ and I no longer live, but Christ lives in me. The life I live in the body, I live by faith in the Son of God, who loved me and gave himself for me.

If you keep on biting and devouring each other, watch out or you will be destroyed by each other. (Galatians 2:20; 5:15)

The Israelites said to Gideon, "Rule over us—you, your son and your grandson—because you have saved us out of the hand of Midian."

But Gideon told them, "I will not rule over you, nor will my son rule over you. The Lord will rule over you."

One day the trees went out to anoint a king for themselves. (Judges 8:22–23; 9:8)

These various passages constitute a composite picture representing with peculiar vividness the nature and malignity of self.

The first thing we see is self-renunciation. This

stands out in the last chapter of Gideon's life. After defeating Israel's enemies, Gideon, by the world's standards, deserves the honor of a crown. But he had the grace and humility to refuse it. As a result, his life ended as it began. It started in nothingness and ended in self-abnegation.

That is not the case with all Christians, though. Some start with God's glorious blessing, then they begin to heap upon themselves honor and glory because of His blessing. In the end their lives become consumed with self-consciousness and fleshly pride.

Saul is an example of this kind of person. His life began in modesty, but it ended in stubborn pride. He stands as a monument of humiliating failure and irretrievable ruin.

The same thing can happen to some noble Christian enterprise we decide to undertake. In the beginning, when it is weak and dependent upon God, it is blessed. But when it becomes strong and successful, it is apt to rise into self-sufficiency and end in world conformity and selfishness. This has been the bane of Christianity in every age.

A republican form of government does not save a people from the kingship of human selfishness. The spirit of social preeminence, political boss-ism and personal ambition runs through all our institutions and social life. Similarly, the Church has lost her power because the disciples are still disputing who should be the greatest. Christ's answer is forever unequivocal and plain, "whoever wants to be first among you, must be your servant" (Matthew 20:27).

Nothing is more important today than to guard the Church of God against the preeminence of men. No wise Christian worker will want to throw the shadow of his own personality too strongly across his work, or become necessary to the success of his cause. Let the secret of our strength be the simple apostolic rule, "you have only one Master and you are all brothers" (Matthew 23:8).

Selfishness leads to ruin

Set off against self-renunciation is self-aggrandizement. Gideon exhibited self-renunciation, but his son did not. The story of Abimelech and the parable of Jotham stand out forever as portraits of self in its most subtle and destructive forms. Abimelech was the illegitimate son of Gideon, born of a Shechemite mother. He seems to have been ostracized from the rest of Gideon's family.

After Gideon's death the spirit of selfish ambition seized Abimelech, and playing on the clannish jealousies of his Shechemite relatives, he persuaded them to crown him as their king. He hired a bunch of mercenaries as the nucleus of his army. With these he attacked his father's home and murdered all his brothers except Jotham, his youngest brother, who succeeded in escaping. After this, he assembled all the people in the valley of Shechem for his coronation.

When Jotham heard what was happening, he climbed a nearby hill and shouted at the crowd, "Listen to me, citizens of Shechem, so that God may listen to you," (Judges 8:7). He then proceeded to tell them a parable about their selecting a king, and none of them mistook his message.

Jotham's parable was a portrait of the meanness and fleshliness of selfishness. At the same time it told in unmistakable language the sequence of events that was sure to follow the crowing of Abimelech as king.

After Abimelech had governed Israel for three years, the prophecy began to unfold. Abimelech and his Shechemite friends became estranged. Treachery met treachery, until it culminated in a revolution against Abimelech. This was followed by warfare until the Shechemites were murdered by the thousands and their city razed.

Abimelech pressed on against his enemies, ravaging with fire and sword until at last he brought his foes to bay in the stronghold of Thebez. Some of this city's people managed to escape to a tower and there made their last stand. Abimelech led the final attack, and as he approached the tower, one of the women defenders dropped a rock on him, crushing his skull. Not wanting his enemy to say that a woman had killed him, Abimelech called for his armor-bearer and told him to kill him with his sword.

Thus, God repaid Abimelech's wickedness. Truly, as Jotham prophesied, fire had come out from the bramble of Abimelech to consume the men of Shechem and, at last, Abimelech.

The fruit of the carnal nature

We see the origin of self-aggrandizement in this account. It is born of the flesh, even as Abimelech was born of the woman of Shechem. Self in all its forms, however subtle and disguised, is the fruit of the carnal nature, and it is the root and center of the sinful life. We cannot cut off our sinful acts and habits until we strike the heart of evil, our self-life, where self is exalted and made king and everything else made tributary to its will, pleasure and honor.

We see, too, that self lives on the selfishness of others and uses the same principle in them for the gratification of its ends. Abimelech appealed to the men of Shechem by ties of race and blood and by the inducements of their own self-interest. Each was bound to the other by selfishness, and Abimelech, knowing best how to play upon the selfish passions of others, makes them subject to his own needs.

We see self in partnership with Satan. Abimelech went to the temple of Baal to secure the finances for his unholy war. The devil is always ready to advance the funds to carry out any scheme of human selfishness. He is a liberal investor in selfish trusts and sinful monopolies. Millions and millions of dollars are being thrown away every day in Satan's investments and sin's cooperative societies, while the cause of Christ languishes.

We see also that the devil not only provides the means but also the men. Abimelech soon found a group of rascals ready to follow him and do his bidding. Unfortunately, there are plenty of such men still to be found. They are the peril of modern society, and some day they will rise in myriad swarms, like the Vandals who swallowed Rome, and capture this world for Satan. And selfishness is ever ready to use them as its minions, and things that some men would not do themselves, they are willing to let these sons of Belial do.

Next we see self unmasking itself and sinking to the depths of cruelty to accomplish its purpose. Abimelech never stopped until his hands were drenched in the blood of his own brothers. He butchered them on the very stone where the angel half a century before had accepted Gideon's offering.

When a burglar enters the house of his victim, his direct object is not to murder, but he is armed for the worst, and if murder is necessary to accomplish his design or to protect himself, he is not going to shirk it. Likewise, when we start out on the pathway of selfishness and sin, only the mercy of God can keep us from doing evil. Well may we all thank God that we have not been allowed to go further than we have.

Empty glory

The sixth thing we see is the foolishness and

shortsightedness of selfishness. How vividly Jotham brought this out in his coronation-day pronouncement! The olive tree did not want to be king because it would cost too much to leave the fatness of its fruit and the richness of its soil for the empty honor of waving over the other trees.

The fig tree, too, had no desire for a glory that would rob it of its sweetness. The vine was too sensible to sacrifice its luscious grapes and its reviving wine, which even God appreciated and which was a blessing to man, for the sake of a brief preeminence over the other trees. The only shrub that was willing to even consider the proposition of royal honors was a thornbush, which had no fruit to sacrifice, no blossoms to lose and no real business in life but to be a nuisance and torment to others.

So the bramble entered into negotiation with the trees. It expressed a little courteous surprise and skepticism about their sincerity in appealing to it and then, with a touch of sarcasm, said, "If you really want to anoint me king over you, come and take refuge in my shade" (Judges 9:15).

The thornbush meant business. If it was to be king, it insisted on the complete subjection of all the other trees under its thorny scepter. But in the next phrase we see that it spoke out its honest thought and intention, "if not, then let fire come out of the thornbush and consume the cedars of Lebanon" (verse 15).

We see how little attraction supremacy had for

the olive tree, the fig tree and the vine. They had something better to do than rule over others. They had a mission of beneficence, sweetness and service.

A man anointed by the Holy Spirit, fed on the sweetness of Christ and bearing fruit for God and man, is not craving after self-aggrandizement. Empty glory can never fill the human heart; vanity and pride are no substitutes for the joy of the Lord, the fullness of the Spirit and the sweet rest we find at Jesus' feet. A life of holy service for others is much more delightful than receiving and seeking their honor.

Let us not be so foolish as to waste our lives in the same pursuits as the thornbush wasted its life. God made us for Himself and for the ministry of love. Let us give no place to self, which is but a sapling out of Satan's root. A thornbush by nature, self has been a curse to us as it will be to everybody else.

The scorpion stings itself

We see the evil fruition of self as it works out in the destiny of others and then reacts in our own destruction. Abimelech's life was the historical fulfillment of Jotham's parable. For a little while the bramble king seemed like an olive or a fig tree. His thorns were not yet fully grown. For three years Abimelech seemed to do well.

Similarly, self hides its sting for a while, and under its nice manners and winning smile, it almost looks like an angel. But when the test comes the thorns appear. The slumbering serpent awakes with its poisonous sting. The men of Shechem had harbored a serpent in their bosom who was now going to kill them. What an awful picture of treachery and destructiveness!

Abimelech oppressed the Shechemites, and they attempted to dethrone him. In turn they were consumed and destroyed by his vengeance. And in the final turn of the wheels of retribution, Abimelech was killed.

How true are the apostle's words, "If you keep on biting and devouring each other, watch out or you will be destroyed by each other" (Galatians 5:15). A selfish spirit is a torment to everybody and at last the greatest curse to itself. Like the scorpion, it spends its life in stinging others, and then at last gathers up itself and with one last effort stings itself to death.

It is not possible for selfishness to make anybody else happy, and it is still less possible for it to make its possessor happy. It is a thornbush by nature, and its end will be the consuming flame.

One of Aesop's fables illustrates this point. A fox fell off a cliff. He reached out and grabbed a thornbush to break his fall and found that it had injured him worse than the fall. He turned to it in anger and disappointment and reproached it for its deceitful cruelty. The bramble honestly replied, "How can anybody expect to catch hold of me, when the business of my life is to catch hold of others?"

May God open our eyes to see the curses of selfishness! If there is one thing in us that seeks for honor and glory, it is a thornbush. And it can only bring us misery and the flames of judgment. Let us repudiate it and follow the life of holy service, finding our rich reward in the sweet, divine joy of holy usefulness.

Nailed to the cross

How can we be saved from the curse of selfishness? Just before God banished Adam and Eve from the Garden of Eden, He issued a decree:

> Cursed is the ground because of you;
>   through painful toil you will eat of it
>   all the days of your life.
> It will produce thorns and thistles for you,
>   and you will eat the plants of the field.
>   (Genesis 3:17–18)

Adam's curse was the fruit of his sin; it was the first outcome of man's fall. The thornbush still stands as a representation of man's sin and God's curse.

Will we make it our king? Will we join hands with Satan, whose own fall began with selfishness and pride? God forbid! Let us turn our backs on it and seek the Tree of Life in the midst of the paradise of God.

Let us remember what cut our Savior's brow on the cross—a crown of thorns. The drops of blood that stained His face and the tears that mingled with them represent the brambles of our selfishness. They are the thorns of our pride. This selfish "I" murdered Christ. It was not only for our sins He died but also for our selfishness. And in that death we die.

That is the secret of victory over self. "We are convinced that one died for all, and therefore all died. And he died for all, that those who live should no longer live for themselves but for him who died for them and was raised again" (2 Corinthians 5:14).

We see, too, the vision of hope in that thorny crown. We see the thorns of our selfishness fastened to His cross, and we know that we as well as our sin are dead indeed. The people we were now no longer exist. They have been nailed to the cross with Christ Jesus. There they hang on the bowed head of our Redeemer. We are new men and women, born out of heaven and united with the risen Christ. "I have been crucified with Christ and I no longer live, but Christ lives in me. The life I live in the body, I live by faith in the Son of God, who loved me and gave himself for me" (Galatians 2:20).

The Faith That Leads
to Faithfulness

His master replied, "Well done, good and faithful servant!" (Matthew 25:21)

The story of Jephthah illustrates two important principles in the divine economy. The first is that God "chose the lowly things of this world and the despised things—and the things that are not—to nullify the things that are, so that no one may boast before him" (1 Corinthians 1:28–29). The second is that God not only wants men who can trust Him, but men whom He can trust.

Jephthah was born a child of misfortune. His father slept with a prostitute, and Jephthah was the result. However, his father was married and had other sons by his wife. Evidently, Jephthah lived with his father's family, because we read in Judges 11:2 that when these other sons grew up, they forced Jephthah to leave. " 'You are not going to get any inheritance in our family,' they said, 'because you are the son of another woman.' "

This kind of rejection would cause bitterness in most people, and Jephthah could easily have said, "What is the use of trying? Everything and everybody is against me. The very heavens are hostile, and either there is no God or there is no God for me. Religion is for the fortunate and favored ones. I am a child of hate. Because everyone is against me, I will be against everyone, except if I can use them for my own advantage."

This would be the typical reaction of human character apart from the grace of God. But grace always proves an exception to every ordinary and natural law. And so we find Jephthah rising above the unfavorable circumstances of his life and developing into a person with character. He wrung strength and success out of the difficulties that threatened to crush him. And he did it not through his own strength but through the grace of God. As we shall see, Jephthah was a man of deep devotion and intense fidelity to God.

A "good" land

We see a bit of Jephthah's character in the name he gave his new home. He called it Tob, which means "good." Jephthah looked at his land in the golden light of faith and hope, and all was bright.

Likewise, God wants His people today to be delivered from sorrow just as much as from sin. Israel's long and sad failure in the wilderness all began in the spirit of discontent and murmuring. From this point they went on to rebellion and judgment—the loss of Canaan and the curse of God.

There is in the spirit of discontent a morbid and unwholesome touch, which is just as defiling as if a person actually had committed a sin. It chills the temperature of the spiritual life and hurts every plant of faith and love. It only takes one frost to destroy the orange crop in Florida, and likewise, one touch of morbidness and selfish, sentimental sorrow will not only chill our own spirit, but it will depress everyone with whom we come in contact. It will lower the temperature of a whole community of happy Christians. Let us live in the "land of Tob," and let us accept the fullness of His atonement. Christ not only bore our sins and sicknesses but our sorrows, too.

Jephthah's name is significant. It means "God opens," and it expresses the kind of trust that looks to Jehovah to open the way and to clear the path of all difficulties and trials.

Unwholesome companions

As we continue in our passage, we read that "a group of adventurers gathered around [Jephthah] and followed him" (Judges 11:3). Because Scripture calls these men "adventurers," we can be sure that they where are not the "cream" of society. They were probably much like Jephthah—individuals who had been thrown out in the sea of life and left to sink or swim. And they naturally gravitated to a stronger center like Jephthah. Such companions are not usually conducive to the development of high, moral character.

How often do we hear people complaining that others have led them astray? But in the Bible we read that the lives of many of God's most faithful servants were molded through the influence of "negative" associations. Joseph grew to honor and obey the Lord despite the godless people around him. David, in his exile years, was surrounded by the outlaws and outcasts of Israel, but through the power of his own personality and the grace of God, these men became transformed into his noblest followers and friends and, afterward, were made the princes of his kingdom.

That is how the Lord Jesus takes us. We were a company of poor, worthless sinners, but by the transforming power of His grace, He lifts us into His own likeness and crowns us with His own glory.

But we have to go back into the world, into a society of evil men. It is our task to lift them up, to bring them to Christ, instead of letting them draw us down. We are to be lights to a dark world.

I once heard a story of a Methodist preacher in England who was arrested and put in jail because of his street preaching. He prayed so loudly that the authorities were glad to get him out. There is no place where we cannot live the life of Christ and receive the glory of His indwelling.

Deliverer

"Some time later, when the Ammonites made war on Israel, the elders of Gilead went to get Jephthah from the land of Tob" (verse 4). Earlier, in verse one of our chapter, Jephthah is called "a mighty warrior." Now, his brothers are in trouble, and they need a mighty warrior to help them out. The people that once despised him, now need his services, and Jephthah has the chance of returning good for evil.

This is the way that God loves to vindicate us— by making us a blessing to those who hated and wronged us. His promise is, "I will make them come and fall down at your feet and acknowledge that I have loved you" (Revelation 3:9).

We see in Jephthah's response the spirit of godliness. All his words to the people were "repeated . . . before the Lord" (Judges 11:11). He spoke as if he were in Jehovah's presence. And when he sent his challenge to the enemy, it was couched in the language of faith. He repelled their claim to some of the land Israel possessed by reminding them how they had treated Israel in the wilderness and had forced a conflict. Then God had taken their land and given it to His own people. "What right have you to take it over?" (verse 23) he finally asked them. "Whatever the Lord our God has given us, we will possess" (verse 24). Jephthah refers the impending conflict once more to Jehovah God.

The battle was not the Israelites but the Lord's.

And, as we read, Jephthah defeated the Ammonites. His country was delivered, his claims vindicated and his enemies destroyed.

The test of faith

But now we see in Jephthah another lesson—one of the sublimest of faith. Before he went into the conflict, he vowed to Jehovah that when he returned in victory, "whatever comes out of the door of my house to meet me . . . will be the Lord's, and I will sacrifice it as a burnt offering" (verse 31).

"When Jephthah returned to his home in Mitzpah, who should come out to meet him but his daughter, . . . She was an only child" (verse 34). Now came the test of faith. As Jephthah realized all that his vow meant, he was overwhelmed with grief. But he did not hesitate in his conviction, nor did his daughter shrink back from the sacrifice imposed upon her. Even she demanded that he fulfill his vow to the Lord.

There have been several interpretations concerning the real meaning of Jephthah's promise to God and the real fate of his daughter. I do not believe that he actually sacrificed his daughter, as the Ammonites sacrificed their children before their god of fire. In Deuteronomy 18, Israel is warned against imitating the cruel and wicked rites of the Ammonites, especially in offering human sacrifices.

Because the Ammonites were the very people against whom Jephthah had gone to war, he would have known better than to consider human sacrifice. For him to directly disobey these solemn injunctions would have been to prove false his character and the meaning of his victory in the name of Jehovah.

No, I think Jephthah sequestered his daughter to protect her virginity and to keep her for the service of the Lord. We read in verse 37 that she requested her father give her time to be with her friends to mourn the fact that she would never marry. If Jephthah was going to put her to death, it is hard to imagine that she would be mourning having no husband—she would be mourning her soon death.

Verse 39 in the King James Version says, "she knew no man. . . . it was a custom in Israel." The first part, "she knew no man," in the original language, is in the future tense. It refers to her future virginity. People thus consecrated to the Lord lived in a state of unchangeable celibacy. From this, I think we can say Jephthah did not kill his daughter, but he made sure she remained a virgin, available for God's service.

The lesson we see here is that what God requires from His people is not a dead body, but a living sacrifice. It is much harder to live for God than to die for Him. It takes much less spiritual and moral power to leap into the conflict and fling a life away in the excitement of the battle than it does to live through 50 years of misunderstanding, pain and temptation.

It would have been far easier for Jephthah's

daughter to die and be buried among the flowers of spring, the chants and songs of a religious ceremonial and the tears and tributes of the people who loved her, knowing that her name would be forever enshrined, than it would have been for her to live as a recluse for God, giving up the dearest hope of every Hebrew woman to be a wife and mother. This was the sacrifice she made.

God is looking for people on whom He can depend. He will put the weight of His highest service and His eternal glory on such men. God help us to be people who, as the Psalmist says, "despises a vile man / but honors those who fear the Lord, / who keeps his oath / even when it hurts," (Psalm 15:4).

Separation and Strength

Therefore come out from them
  and be separate,
says the Lord.
Touch no unclean thing,
  and I will receive you.
(2 Corinthians 6:17)

The story of Samson is an illustration of this text. Here we see divine strength mingled with human weakness, supernatural power hindered by the touch of earth and the taint of sin.

Samson's story forms one of the closing chapters of the period of the judges. As the account unfolds, we read that an angel of the Lord came to Manoah's wife, who was sterile, saying that she would soon give birth to a son. Along with this news came a solemn pronouncement:

> Now see to it that you drink no wine or other fermented drink and that you do not eat anything unclean, because you will con-

74

ceive and give birth to a son. No razor may be used on his head, because the boy is to be a Nazirite, set apart to God from birth, and he will begin the deliverance of Israel from the hands of the Philistines. (Judges 13:4)

In due time the child was born and carefully brought up according to the divine command. His hair was allowed to grow, and he abstained from wine and lived a life of abstinence and purity. When he reached manhood the Spirit of God came upon him in the form of extraordinary physical strength. But along with this came the temptation of his life—a tendency to self-indulgence and a lust for Philistine women. And these became the snare that ruined him.

His first error was to fall in love with a young Philistine woman of Timnath and to marry her contrary to the advice and wishes of his parents. This marriage ended in the murder of his bride and the family by the Philistines. Samson retaliated by burning up their cornfields by sending an army of blazing foxes across the country.

For 20 years he was the terror of his enemies. He defied their attempts to take him—until he fell in love with Delilah. After winning his confidence, she tricked him into revealing the secret of his strength. Delilah then cut off his hair and delivered him to her countrymen, who bound him, put out his eyes and then placed him in a solitary dungeon.

There his hair began to grow again, and the

strength of the Lord returned to him. Some time later, the Philistines gathered to offer a great sacrifice to their god, Dagon, and to celebrate the capture of Samson. They mocked him, making him perform for them. As he stood among the pillars of the temple, he asked the servant who led him around to place him next to the two main columns that supported the temple. Then he prayed to God,

> O Sovereign Lord, remember me. O God, please strengthen me just once more, and let me with one blow get revenge on the Philistines for my two eyes. (Judges 16:28)

Samson then pushed the columns with all his strength and the temple came crashing down, killing more people with this one blow than he had done in his entire life.

And so he passed out of Jewish history—a marvelous example of what God might have done with a completely separated man, and yet of what self-indulgence and sin can do to hinder the glorious promise and the gracious purpose of God.

A bright beginning

Samson's life had a bright beginning. It was full of promise and possibility. God chose him and planned out his life with a divine purpose. But Samson was defeated by earthliness, selfishness and sin.

What more could God have done to show His purpose of love and blessing? Twice He sent His angel to announce the birth of Samson. Time after time He manifested His supernatural power in the life of His servant. Yet all this was brought to nothing by the disobedience and folly of the man whom He had sought to bless and use.

It is an awful thing to think that we can hinder God's purposes for us. This is an important lesson. Despite the fact that we may have been born to Christian parents who brought us up to fear God; despite the fact that our early days were overshadowed by the Almighty and our consciousnesses felt the touch of heaven and heard the whisper of His calling on our lives; we may, by our willfulness and folly, destroy all this. Sad will be the day when we hear our Master say, as He said of Jerusalem, "how often I have longed to gather your children together, as a hen gathers her chicks under her wings, but you were not willing" (Matthew 23:37).

No other way

We see in Samson's story the necessity for a life of separation and consecration. There is no other way the Holy Spirit can work in our lives; there is no other way we can become the instruments of God's highest blessing.

The Nazirite, under Mosaic law, was supposed to lead a life of separation. He was set apart from his childhood to be dedicated to the Lord and separated from all earthly and sensual indulgences. Just as the priest represented the idea of nearness to God, the Nazirite represented the idea of separation to God.

This is a key principle in God's plan of redemption. From the beginning God purposed to separate a people to Himself. We see this in the separation of Abel, Noah, Abraham, Isaac, Israel and others down to the Church of Christ. The name Ekklesia means "the separated ones." Man's failure to meet God's ideal has been the cause of all the failures and disasters of the past.

The awful wickedness that preceded the flood was brought about from the intermarriage of the children of God with the daughters of man. And today the same cause is about to produce similar effects. There is a melting away and a breaking down of all barriers between the Church and the world, and the end of it is going to be conditions as shocking and terrible as those of Noah's day. The progeny of such frightful and monstrous unions will once more bring upon the earth a deluge—not of water, but of fire—and the godless will be swept away.

God must have separated vessels. He will not drink out of the devil's cups. We must be His and His alone. We must bear His monogram and be His peculiar people.

If you are claiming to be a Christian but still playing with the world, you are opening the floodgates for a coming judgment. You are contaminating the Body of Christ with the poison of your sin. You are draining the fountains of spiritual life and power and, in effect, repeating the story of Samson. And the end can only be the same as his—blindness, bondage, paralysis and death.

Not a physical giant

We see in Samson a picture of the supernatural life and power that God can give to a consecrated human body. There is no reason to suppose that Samson was a physical giant. The Philistines could not understand his supernatural strength. If he had been like Og or Sihon or Goliath—men of gigantic stature—they would easily have comprehended it. But he seems to have been a man of ordinary appearance.

His power, as Scripture tells us, was supernatural. It did not come from physical prowess. No, it was a result of the divine life that possessed his being and filled his frame.

I am reminded here of another biblical figure who was endowed with divine strength—David. We read often that he attributed his stupendous exploits to the abilities that came to him from Jehovah. His battles were battles of faith, and he could literally say, "He trains my hands for battle; / my arms can bend a bow of bronze" (2 Samuel 22:35). We have seen the power of demon possession in a human body. Why should not the Holy Spirit be able to give the same power to a human arm?

Samson was able to tear apart a lion with his bare hands. He killed 1,000 men with the jawbone of a donkey. He carried the pillars and city gate of Gaza on his back to the top of a hill. And, as his last act of strength, he pushed down the columns that supported the temple of Dagon.

God can do the same thing in one of us. He could endue us with the power to resist disease, to persevere under the influence of a harsh climate, to endure hardship and suffering and to go through life, like Moses, with unabated strength until our work is finished.

The Holy Spirit has this for His separated ones in these last days. It is part of the purchase of Christ's redemption and the partnership of His resurrection and ascension power. And if we are empty of all that hinders and open to His unrestricted life and power, He will dwell in us and fill us with His great power.

We see more than physical strength in Samson's life; we also see God's supernatural working in the circumstances of life. When Samson was ready to faint from thirst after his victory over the Philistines, he cried to God, and God opened a fountain of water from which Samson could drink.

True faith can always claim the interposition of God in all the emergencies and circumstances of life. While the Spirit dwells within us as the source of every needed grace, the Son of God is reigning at His Father's right hand. He said to His disciples, "All authority in heaven and on earth has been given to me. . . . And surely I am with you always, to the very end of the age" (Matthew 28:18–20). This mighty Christ is able to do anything for us that we really need in the line of His purpose for us and the work He has committed to our hands.

A gradual fall

We see, too, the withering touch of earthliness and sin. Samson's fall was a gradual one. Temptation wove its web around him slowly, until at last he was a bound and helpless captive in the power of his destroyer.

His first offense was a visit to the enemy's country. He had no business in going down to Timnath to start with, except as God might send him as a soldier or as a judge. But he went anyway, and while there he fell in love with a Philistine woman. Nothing would do him until he married her—against his parents' counsel— taking the fatal step that linked his life with the daughter of his enemy.

God did not forsake Samson immediately. He showed His power through His servant over a number of years and helped him out of a multitude of troubles. No doubt God often spoke to Samson and warned him of his folly. But Samson continued down the same self-indulgent path, getting deeper and deeper into sin. At last we find him at Gaza in the house of a prostitute, Delilah, who represents the world's delights and abandonment to selfish pleasure.

Even there an instinct of self-preservation remained with Samson. This woman, Satan's masterpiece of temptation, had been paid by her rulers to find out the secret of Sampson's strength. Using her female charms, she begged Samson to tell her his secret. "How can you say, 'I love you,' when you won't confide in me?" she said to him (Judges 16:15). At last, Samson gave in.

Perhaps you have found yourself in a similar situation. You never intended to yield your principles, your virtue, your conscience, but this person convinced you to do just that. And in one impulsive moment, you were lost.

That is how Samson fell. He knew there was danger, and he played with it, day by day, putting it off and still holding the citadel. But with each day, the enemy came closer and closer. First, he told Delilah that if he were to be tied with seven fresh thongs then he would be as weak as any other man. Next, he told her it actually took new ropes. Then it was braiding his hair into a loom. Then, finally, the truth came out. God's hour of long-suffering had passed, and the man who might have been a lighthouse on the shores of time, became instead a beacon on the sunken rock, a warning to others to avoid the place where he was lost.

In the end, the strong man bowed, the surrender was made and the secret was told. The awful progression was completed. Lust had been conceived and brought forth sin. And sin, when it was finished, brought death (James 1:15).

Spiritual paralysis

Samson's retribution was as terrible as his sin. He lost his strength, and spiritual paralysis always follows surrender to temptation and compromise with evil. Next, he lost his liberty. He was bound and helpless in the hands of his foes. When once we yield to the enemy, we have no power to keep from yielding again. Our defense is departed from us, and we are given over "to a depraved mind, to do what ought not to be done" (Romans 1:28). Eternal sin is the most terrible part of eternal punishment.

Samson lost his sight. When we yield to sin, our spiritual eyes are blinded, and we cease to know the difference between right and wrong. Our once clear conceptions of God's will are blurred and blotted out, and we wander in the darkness.

He became a spectacle for his enemies. They used him to grace their entertainments, and his downfall was held up for all to see. And the most terrible part of Samson's punishment was to hear the shouts of his enemies as they boasted of the triumphs of Dagon over Jehovah and the defeat of Samson and Samson's God. All the while, though, Samson knew it was his sin and folly that caused this shame to the name of Jehovah—the name he, above all men, was sent to uphold.

In the end, Samson was repentant. In his humiliation, bondage and sorrow, he awoke at last to the meaning of his life, and he asked God for one more chance to be true. To prove his sincerity, he was willing to sacrifice his life in his last exploit.

Our service is never worth anything until our life goes along with it and everything is laid down, even life itself if God requires it. Samson had sought only his own pleasure his whole life. But in the end he died to self and, in doing so, accomplished the noblest achievement of his life.

Let us learn from this story to die to self and sin. If we can do so, then we will be like those individuals of the Old Testament "whose weakness was turned to strength; and who became powerful in battle and routed foreign armies" (Hebrews 11:34). Let us see in Samson's death the lesson of how to live and how to die.

Religious Compromises

No one can serve two masters. Either he will hate the one and love the other, or he will be devoted to the one and despise the other. You cannot serve both God and Money. (Matthew 6:24)

The remarkable incidents of Judges 17 and 18 illustrate the principles found in Matthew 6:24. They contain the story of Micah and are a medley of sin and crime that condemn with the bitter irony of truth the follies and sins of the dark ages of the Judges. And they apply to the social and religious abuses of our own times.

First, we see a picture of dishonesty. Micah, a young man of Mount Ephraim, stole 1,100 shekels of silver from his mother and, for a time, hid the money from her. Finally, alarmed by her angry curses, he confessed that he had taken the money, and he gave it back to her.

This a common happening—dishonesty and crime beginning at home with the first penny stolen from mother's drawer. From this the person goes on to lead a life of lawlessness and crime.

Absolute righteousness even in the smallest of things is essential to all religious character. We find a lack of righteousness today in society's concepts of right and wrong. There are men and women who can speak of deep religious experiences and extraordinary public services, who yet seem to be unable to appreciate the absolute necessity of strict integrity and uprightness in the matter of property, debt and business transactions.

Next, we see a picture of passion. When Micah's mother found that her money was missing, she became angry. Her curses made such an impression on Micah that he confessed to being the thief. The moment the shekels were returned, she forgot about her anger and about the fact that Micah had taken them. She was so happy to have her money back that she probably forgot about punishing Micah. Instead, she blessed him.

Worthless religion

As we continue in the account, we see a picture of counterfeit consecration. "I solemnly consecrate my silver to the Lord for my son to make a carved image and a cast idol" (Judges 17:3). What a strange medley of religion and idolatry! Micah's mother had "religion," but it was worthless.

The world's need is not religion; there is plenty of it to go around. In fact, the less a man has of God the more he has of religion. Animists in Africa or Hindus in India have far more religion than Christians in North America. They sacrifice, give and do more in the service of their gods than we do for Christ—but their's is the devil's religion.

Back of all their idolatry they, like Micah's mother, have a dim idea of the Lord. They will tell you that these images and fetishes are but forms and stepping stones through which they can rise to the true God. They have a sense that there is a God, and they desire to meet Him. But this does not make their practices any more acceptable. The motive does not make the act right.

Similarly, we may have much piety in building our chapels, in erecting our altars, in contributing to the costly machinery of our splendid rituals and in keeping our fasts and our Lenten services, but it is idolatry all the same. It will be a sad day for many "devoted worshipers" when they find that God has accepted none of their foolish sacrifices, and that all their expenditure of money, time and bodily exercise has been as vain as the Muslim's prayers to Mecca.

Notice, though, in this woman's consecration, how she betrayed herself by an act of insincerity in the midst of her pretended sacrifice. "I solemnly consecrate my silver to the Lord," she said. Yet when it came to actually giving up the money, she only took out 200 shekels. She kept the rest for herself—she was not even honest in the little religion she had.

How natural it is to let self come into our devotions. We need to heed the admonition of Paul:

"Now finish the work, so that your eager willingness to do it may be matched by your completion of it, according to your means" (2 Corinthians 8:11).

Man-made religion

We see too a picture of ritualism. Micah's mother had the image made and gave it to him to set up in his house. He "had a shrine, and he made an ephod and some idols and installed one of his sons as his priest" (Judges 17:5).

Micah's religion was manufactured according to his own patterns—not God's. And this is the essential defect of all forms of false religion—they are man-made. Their basic fault is that they are human, that they are based upon the traditions or inventions of man and not upon the revealed Word and authoritative commandment of Jehovah.

God's command to Moses was that he should do all that was told him according to the patterns shown him on the mountain. Christ's command to His disciples asserted the same notion: "Therefore go . . . and teach them to obey everything I have commanded you" (Matthew 28:19–20). But Satan has tried to institute into the Church a whole system of theological teaching and ceremonial worship that God never revealed or commanded and to change the whole divine system into a piece of human machinery that he could manipulate at will.

How much of our religious work today is entirely human? Our revivals are carefully organized with little thought of what God would have us do. Our worship services have become static rituals. And much of our so-called religion is what Scripture describes as "teachings . . . taught by men" (Matthew 15:9) and as things that "are all destined to perish with use, because they are based on human commands and teachings" (Colossians 2:22).

After Micah had set up his "temple," he felt as if something was lacking. He wanted God to recognize his man-made church to give it a touch of authority and sacredness. One day a young man from Bethlehem came by Micah's house looking for a place to live. Micah, discovering that he was a Levite, asked him to come live with him and be his priest. He offered him a salary of 10 shekels a year, his clothing and his room and board.

The young man accepted and was installed as the hired preacher in Micah's church. Micah had just enough of God in his man-made church to justify his calling it a religious institution. He said with delightful self-complacency, "Now I know that the Lord will be good to me, since this Levite has become my priest" (Judges 17:13).

In the same way men and women today are making up their various religious programs, wanting only to get ecclesiastical recognition, to get some Levite with real apostolic succession to countenance the thing. It does not matter whether God approves or disapproves.

I have seen men with liberal minds and attractive personalities go forth as teachers, winning the confidence and acclaim of many Christians. Their creeds are so tactfully phrased that they are accepted by Unitarians, Jews, Spiritualists—as well as Christians. These men could stand as representatives of the most conservative of the churches and be recognized as true Levites.

And I have seen men who, with the wild license of modern theological thought and the passion for freedom and originality, have literally excised every supernatural thing from the Bible. Yet somehow these same individuals manage to secure the highest places in our theological seminaries. They are recognized as star lecturers at our Christian conventions. And no one seems to challenge their positions.

I know too of churches that use their sanctuaries—the temples of God—as places for religious entertainments and exhibitions, some of which would not even be considered decent on Broadway. Their schedules include the weekly dance as well as the weekly prayer meeting. And somehow, they are able to justify it all as scriptural. The members and officers of this man-made medley fold their arms in self-complacency, like Micah, and say, "It is all right. We have a 'man of God' as our pastor."

The end results
Finally, we see a picture of the sad fruits of religious compromise.

> The tribe of the Danites was seeking a place of their own where they might settle, because they had not yet come into an inheritance among the tribes of Israel. So the Danites sent five warriors from Zorah and Eshtaol to spy out the land and explore it. (Judges 18:1–2)

This band came to the house of Micah and spent the night. They recognized Micah's young priest, and after finding out what he was doing there, they asked him to inquire of God about whether their mission would be successful. The priest told them, "Go in peace. Your journey has the Lord's approval" (verse 6).

They continued on their journey, and finding a prosperous land, they returned home and urged their people to arm for battle. The army set out, stopping first at Micah's house. There they stole his priest and his gods.

When Micah found out what had happened, he and his clan went after the Danites. "As they shouted after them, the Danites turned and said to Micah, 'What's the matter with you that you called out your men to fight?' " (verse 23). Seeing that he was overmatched, Micah turned around and went back home. The Danites marched on with their booty and invaded the city of Laish. They then set up their own idolatrous shrine and seat of worship, which became in succeeding years the most corrupting influence in the religious life of the entire nation.

Here we see the effects that always accompany religious compromise. It leads to the bitter disappointment of the worshiper. All of Micah's glorious plans were swept away in an instant, and he was left with nothing but scorn and despair.

The leaven of false religion also becomes a corrupting principle in succeeding generations. Micah not only corrupted his own family; he laid the foundation of sin that lasted for years into the future.

When we defile the streams of divine truth and life, we poison a whole generation. When we plant weeds with the wheat, we leave behind seeds of thorns and thistles. We may think it is OK to play with "higher criticism" and ritualism, but doing so will undermine the faith of our children and our children's children. We are kindling the fire that will burn up our altars and homes. And we are pioneering the awful procession of anarchy, socialism, immorality, crime and the horrors of lawlessness and wrong that will usher in the days of Antichrist and the catastrophe of the world.

Our Kinsman-Redeemer

For your Maker is your husband—
the Lord Almighty is his name—
the Holy One of Israel is your Redeemer;
he is called the God of all the earth.
(Isaiah 54:5)

The book of Ruth can be considered as a
part of Judges. It is a vignette inserted on
the background of that mingled picture of the
dark ages of the Old Testament. As such, it is a
companion picture to the story of Micah. Both
are incidents gathered out of the same period of
Hebrew history, and they illustrate the life of the
people—the one the dark side, the other the
bright.

But before we look at Ruth, we should briefly
consider the shocking series of incidents recorded
in the last three chapters of Judges—all of which
grew out of a single unholy relationship. These
chapters tell the story of a licentious woman
destroyed by the wickedness she pursued, and of a
sinful man who allowed her to draw him into her

wicked life, and who, through her influence, became unfaithful to his high calling as a priest of the Lord. Out of their relationship grew a crime that involved all the tribes of Israel in a destructive civil war—a war that destroyed three armies and nearly one whole tribe.

We see from this that even the smallest sin can produce the most disastrous results. How solemn and true is the verse in James: "Then, after desire has conceived, it gives birth to sin; and sin, when it is full-grown, gives birth to death" (James 1:15).

An oasis in the desert

Now we come to the story of Ruth. It is like an oasis in the desert. The German poet Goethe has called it the finest poem in human language, and yet how few of us really understand its beautiful meaning and teaching.

We need only to briefly recall the incidents of the story: the famine in Bethlehem and the emigrant family, Elimelech and his wife Naomi, with their two boys, Mahlon and Chilion. Then came the death of the father and the marriage of the two sons to two women of Moab, Ruth and Orpah. Next, the two sons died, and the three widows were left alone in a foreign land.

Naomi decided to return to her home in Judah, but she tried to dissuade her daughters-in-law from following her, from a journey that promised so little for them. Orpah, the more demonstrative of the two, expressed great affection, and went home. But Ruth clung to Naomi, telling her,

Don't urge me to leave you or to turn back from you. Where you go I will go, and where you stay I will stay. Your people will be my people and your God my God. Where you die I will die, and there I will be buried. May the Lord deal with me, be it ever so severely, if anything but death separates you and me. (Ruth 1:16–17)

So the two traveled to Bethlehem. Ruth took upon herself the support of Naomi and went out like other Jewish young women to glean in the wheat and barley fields. It was there that she met Boaz, the rich farmer, who had heard of her kindness to her mother-in-law. He became attracted to her, showing her special kindness without sacrificing her independence.

Naomi took notice of the unfolding situation, recognizing that Boaz, being her close relative, was their "kinsman-redeemer." It was his duty to redeem her husband's inheritance and take his widow to be his wife. Naomi advised Ruth to take the step by which she could claim her rights.

The sequel, we all know. Boaz recognized the claim, but kindly told her that there was another who was before him. If, however, this man would refuse to do the kinsman's part, Boaz would follow through. The other kinsman declined, and Boaz kept his word. He redeemed the inheritance of Elimelech and took Ruth as his bride. Out of this union came the birth of Obed, the father of

Jesse, the father of David. And thus Ruth, a Moabite, became the grandmother of David, and the ancestress of Jesus Christ, the Son of man, and the King of kings!

Virtuous character

The first thing we notice in this story are the fine examples of virtuous character. Naomi was a true mother. She considered Ruth as her own child and sought her best interests, thereby gaining her confidence and love.

In Ruth we see a genuine love toward her mother-in-law. But we also see a woman of true modesty. What a perfect combination! Modesty is a woman's finest jewel. It is her most attractive quality in the eyes of every true man. This was what drew Boaz to Ruth. She did not chase after the younger men, but stayed with Naomi and worked in the fields.

We see too that Ruth was an industrious woman. She was not afraid of hard work. Boaz recognized and respected this in her, and though he desired to help and did so by telling his men to leave behind some of the stalks, his help maintained her independence.

But above all is the piety of Ruth. It was not only the love of Naomi that made her true, but it was the love of Naomi's God. "May you be richly rewarded by the Lord, the God of Israel, under whose wings you have come to take refuge" (2:12).

Boaz exhibits some outstanding character attributes also. He was wealthy and influential, but he worked his fields alongside his men. He recognized Ruth's situation and acted in kindness toward her. He did just enough to encourage her, but not enough to damage her self-respect.

And he acted justly in his relation to Naomi. Boaz was ready to carry through with his obligation as her kinsman-redeemer, yet at the same time he knew that another man had first rights. Boaz gave this man the chance to claim these rights, even though his own heart was interested in Ruth.

Divine providence

The next thing we see in this story is a beautiful illustration of divine providence. We see God working in human affairs to carry out His divine purpose. We see Him overruling the sorrow of former days to bring about a greater blessing. We see Him leading this daughter of a Gentile race and making her a partner in the hopes of His people. We see Him fitting the times and seasons of our lives in bringing these wanderers back to Bethlehem just at the right time, the harvest season. We see His loving care for His children expressed in Boaz. Under His sheltering wings His children still lie. And through each perplexing path of life, He will guide their footsteps, providing for their need and safely leading them home.

We see too a type of redemption. In the helpless condition of Ruth, we see our lost condition.

Ruth was born of a Gentile race, the Moabites, a race that was under a curse. Moab literally means "son of his father," and we know that the tribe was descended from the union of Lot and his daughter. As such, Ruth well represents the sinful state of God's redeemed people under the curse of a fallen race.

Not only was Ruth a Gentile and a stranger, but she was a widow. Her natural protector was gone, and her nearest kinsman, who had the right to redeem her, refused. How well she represents our helpless condition.

But in contrast to all this is the picture of redemption. Under Mosiac law, there is a statute providing for what are called Levirate marriages, under whose provisions a family name was not allowed to perish from the tribe. When a man died, his brother was to take his wife, have children by her and redeem his inheritance. This, of course, involved the forfeiture of the kinsman's own family name and marred his inheritance, but it was recognized as a patriotic and social duty.

This is what Boaz did for Ruth and what the nearer kinsman refused to do. Boaz merged his own personality and family into Ruth's family, making a real sacrifice, and thus he became her kinsman-redeemer.

And this is what our Kinsman-Redeemer, Jesus Christ, did for us! He sacrificed His own divine rights:

Who, being in very nature God,

did not consider equality with God
  something to be grasped
but made himself nothing,
  taking the very nature of a servant,
  being made in human likeness.
And being found in appearance as a man,
  he humbled himself
  and became obedient to death—
    even death on a cross!
    (Philippians 2:6–8)

Christ gave up a place of dignity and position in heaven, where He was known as God and God alone. And now, He is forever known as man, still divine, yet not exclusively divine, but united to the person, flesh and form of a created being. His whole inheritance is merged in ours. He laid down His rights and honors and took up our wrongs and reproaches, our liabilities and disabilities, and henceforth He has nothing but His people.

He is the merchant man seeking pearls, who, having found one pearl of great price, sold all that He had and bought that pearl. The Church, His Bride, is all He owns. He has invested everything in us. The Lord's portion is His people. Therefore, let us make up to Him what He has laid down. Let us understand His sacrifice and love. And let Him find in us His sufficient and everlasting recompense.

The redeemer not only sacrificed his own inheritance, but he brought back the forfeited inheritance of the dead husband. Likewise, our Kinsman-Redeemer has brought back for us all that we lost in Adam and has added to it infinitely more—all the fullness of His grace, all the riches of His glory, all that the ages to come are yet to unfold in His mighty plan, victory over death, the restoration of the divine image, sonship with God, triumph over Satan, a world restored to more than Eden's blessedness and beauty, the crowns and thrones of the kingdom and all the exceeding riches of His grace and kindness. All this and more is the purchase of His redemption.

But the best of all the blessings brought by our Kinsman-Redeemer is Himself. When Boaz bought the inheritance of Elimelech, he took Ruth also, and she became his bride. And so our Kinsman-Redeemer is also our Husband. Not only does He come down into our nature in the incarnation, but He takes us up into His person in the relationship that is to reach its consummation in the marriage supper of the Lamb.

Faith that dares to claim

We see in Ruth's example the pattern of faith that dares to claim and enter into all the possibilities of its inheritance. It was a bold move on Ruth's part to claim her rights under the Levirate law. She followed Naomi's advice and put herself at the feet of Boaz, in the place to which she was entitled. She left upon him the responsibility of accepting or refusing her.

Her act was the abandonment of faith. But faith

must always abandon itself before it can claim its blessing. We see the same type of faith in Mary, the mother of Jesus. She risked her reputation on the angel's message and believed for the blessing that was to bring the world its Redeemer. "I am the Lord's servant. . . . May it be to me as you have said" (Luke 1:38). And the answer came back, "Blessed is she who has believed that what the Lord has said to her will be accomplished!" (verse 45).

Likewise, faith must always claim its promised rights. Every victory costs a venture, and the blessing is in proportion to the cost. Faith must still see its inheritance under the promise and then step boldly forward and take what God has given. Salvation is not now bestowed as mercy to a pauper, but is claimed in Jesus' name by a trusting child who inherits under his Brother's will.

That is how we take His forgiveness and how we must take every blessing and answer to our prayer all along the way. God has given us the right to take this place of boldness. We are not presuming, but we are honoring His Word. We are not entering beyond our rights, but we are showing our confidence in our Father's truth and love by daring to take all He has dared to give. Let us have boldness to enter into the holiest by the blood of Jesus.

The fruit of faith
Finally, we see that the fruit of Boaz and Ruth's marriage was the dynasty of David and the birth

of Jesus Christ. Ruth's faith brought her into a family of princes and a kingdom of glory. And so for us, too, redemption means a crown and a throne at the Master's glorious coming.

But behind the throne and the crown lies the story of redemption and the bold appropriation of faith. We must learn to know the Bridegroom now if we would sit with Him upon His throne then and share the glory of His millennial reign. Shall we take Him as our Redeemer, our Husband and our coming Lord, and have Him say to us,

> For your Maker is your husband—
>   the Lord Almighty is his name—
> the Holy One of Israel is your Redeemer;
>   he is called the God of all the earth.
>   (Isaiah 54:5)

For more copies of
Danger Lines in the Deeper Life
or information on other Simpson titles available
from Christian Publications, contact your local
Christian bookstore or call toll-free,
1-800-233-4443.

Books by Dr. A.B. Simpson:

The Best of A.B. Simpson
Christ in the Tabernacle
The Christ Life
The Self-Life and the Christ-Life
The Cross of Christ
Days of Heaven on Earth
The Fourfold Gospel
The Gentle Love of the Holy Spirit
The Gospel of Healing
The Holy Spirit Vol. 1
The Holy Spirit Vol. 2
A Larger Christian Life
The Life of Prayer
Missionary Messages
Wholly Sanctified